I0519327

Angela Bell

Along with 5 Other Inspiring Women

MOM MAGIC

Moms Mastering Affiliate & Network Marketing

Table of Contents

INTRODUCTION

The Inspired & Profitable Mompreneur was created by Angela Bell, to serve the need she saw and experienced as a mom; the need for time & financial freedom and flexibility. This need was all the more emphasized during the pandemic, when Moms around the world overloaded by the ever-changing demands brought on by school & daycare closures, working from home, sick and fragile family members needing care, and communities needing love & support. She saw the need for moms to have the ability to continue making money, while simultaneously having flexible schedules and work autonomy. Then, in 2021, she launched a podcast & online TV Show of the same name.

With the goal of showcasing, highlighting, and empowering Moms and Mompreneurs around the world, The Inspired & Profitable Mompreneur Podcast & TV Show serves as a platform for women to spread their message and knowledge, while also being a collection of resources for those who need them. It is now one of the most sought out Mom based podcasts both nationally and internationally. You can find it on your favorite podcast platforms, such as Spotify, Google Podcasts, Apple Podcasts, IHeartRadio, and much more!

The Inspired & Profitable Mompreneur Community on Facebook, serves as a place where current and aspiring Mompreneurs can come together, share resources, support and encourage each other and seek guidance. Knowing that only moms can understand the unique needs and struggles of other moms, Angela is working to create an employer/job seeker sight, to match up Moms looking to grow their team with moms looking for flexible "mom-friendly" work.

Wanting to do more to elevate the status of Moms and Mompreneurs, Angela created the Mom Magic Anthology Series. This series will change the narrative around Moms in entrepreneurship, the work place, and life!

MOMS are the MAGIC in everything around us...

MOM Magic

The Magic of Motherhood and how it's changing the world!

This is for the moms who feel lost, exhausted, overwhelmed, and unacknowledged. For the moms who had dreams, and have put them on the back shelf. For the moms who know they have greatness inside of them, if they could only find a minute. We hear you! We see you! We are you!! This book series was created for you, so you know you are not alone, you are a great mom, and there is a way!!

The women in these books have struggled, lived and thrived in motherhood. They have made peace with the judgment and insane expectations of society, and they have found a way to live their best life! If they can do it, I promise you, SO CAN YOU!! The stories, tools and methods shared in this book and the ones to follow, are a guide to help you live your best life too.

Mom Magic - Unleash the Magic of Network and Affiliate Marketing!!

Discover the path to financial empowerment with **"Mom Magic - Moms Mastering Network and Affiliate Marketing."** Curated by Angela Bell and a team of exceptional authors, this anthology demystifies network and affiliate marketing, showcasing the true potential for moms seeking flexibility and independence.

Explore the benefits:

Flexibility: Earn while raising children, without the constraints of daycare.

Financial Freedom: Start your own business without debt, with comprehensive training included.

Diverse Opportunities: Choose from a variety of companies aligned with your values.

Skill Development: Network marketing becomes a platform for personal growth and skill acquisition.

Community and Relationships: Forge lasting connections with like-minded individuals.

Embark on a transformative journey where mastering network and affiliate marketing becomes the key to a brighter, more fulfilling future. Join us in "Mom Magic" and unlock the secrets to success in the dynamic world of entrepreneurial moms.

By you grabbing this book, it shows that you, too, are ready to show the world your **MOM MAGIC.**

The Inspired & Profitable Mompreneur offers:

- Inspired & Profitable Mompreneur Business Creation Packages
- Inspired & Profitable Mompreneur Podcast
- Mompreneur Launch School
- Mompreneur Mastermind Group
- Inspired & Profitable Mompreneur Community

Moms are the key to creating a better, bright and more compassionate future for us all.

Mom Magic IS the Future...

With Love,
Angela Bell
The Inspired & Profitable Mompreneur

Angela Bell

Founder & CEO of The Inspired & Profitable Momprenuer

https://www.linkedin.com/in/angela-bell-776a529/
https://www.facebook.com/angela.bell.3597/
https://www.instagram.com/i.am.angelabell/
https://www.inspirednprofitablemompreneur.com/

Angela Bell is the founder of The Mom Magic Anthology Series and the Mom Magic Movement! She is also the founder and CEO at The Inspired & Profitable Mompreneur Business, Podcast, Magazine & TV Show.

Angela is on a mission to empower moms around the world to stand in their power, embrace their dreams, and create their own business!

Angela is a 6X International Best Seller, multi-passionate entrepreneur, business coach for moms, and mom of twins.

EMPOWERING MOMS THROUGH AFFILIATE AND NETWORK MARKETING

By Angela Bell

I'll be honest, I am not a successful network or affiliate marketer. While I have tried a few times, it's just not my strong point. That being said, I do strongly believe that these opportunities can be great vehicles for moms looking to create income while maintaining the flexibility mom-life often requires.

It frustrates me to see so many negative posts and comments about MLMs and other types of network and affiliate marketing opportunities. In a world inundated with diverse business opportunities, affiliate marketing, and network marketing have emerged as powerful avenues for individuals seeking financial independence and flexibility. While not everyone may find success in these fields, it's crucial to recognize the unique advantages they offer, especially for moms. Here I would like to shed light on the positive aspects of affiliate and network marketing, challenging the misconceptions that often surround these business models. By doing so, empowering moms to explore these opportunities with a renewed perspective, understanding the potential benefits they can bring.

The Power of Affiliate Marketing for Moms

Affiliate marketing operates on a simple yet effective premise—leveraging affiliates to amplify product or service awareness online, leading to commissions from resulting sales or leads. This model has proven to be a game-changer for moms looking to balance their professional and personal lives.

One of the most significant advantages of affiliate marketing for moms is the flexibility it offers. Unlike traditional 9-to-5 jobs, affiliate marketers have the freedom to set their own schedules. This is particularly beneficial for mothers juggling childcare responsibilities, school commitments, and household chores. The ability to work from home or any location with an internet connection empowers moms to build a career around their family's needs.

Starting a business often requires a substantial financial investment, which can be a deterrent for many individuals, especially moms with limited resources. Affiliate marketing, however, boasts low start-up costs. Affiliates typically don't need to create products, manage inventory, or handle customer service. This minimizes the financial risk associated with entrepreneurship, making it an accessible option for moms looking to venture into the business world.

For moms who are already active on social media or maintain a blog, affiliate marketing provides an opportunity to monetize their existing platforms. By partnering with companies and promoting relevant products or services, moms can earn commissions for each sale generated through their unique affiliate links. This aligns with the current trend of influencers and content creators turning their online presence into a source of income.

Affiliate marketing encourages continuous learning and skill development. Moms involved in affiliate marketing often enhance their digital marketing skills including content creation, search engine optimization (SEO), and social media management. These skills not only contribute to their success in affiliate marketing but also have broader applicability in the ever-evolving digital landscape.

Network Marketing as a Vehicle for Mompreneurs

While affiliate marketing thrives in the digital realm, network marketing capitalizes on person-to-person sales within a distributor network. Successful moms in network marketing have transformed into advanced sales professionals, building legitimate businesses and reshaping the narrative around this often-misunderstood industry.

Network marketing relies heavily on building relationships, and who better to leverage existing relationships than moms? Moms, by nature, are often skilled at connecting with others, whether it's fellow parents at school, neighbors, or friends. This personal touch in sales can be a powerful catalyst for success in network marketing.

One key aspect that sets network marketing apart is the sense of community and mentorship it provides. Moms entering this field often find themselves surrounded by like-minded individuals who understand the challenges and aspirations of balancing family life with entrepreneurship. The mentorship structure within network marketing empowers moms to learn from those who have achieved success, fostering a supportive environment for personal and professional growth.

Network marketing offers a unique compensation structure that rewards both individual sales efforts and team-building activities. Moms can earn commissions not only from their personal sales but also from the sales generated by the team they recruit and support. This creates a scalable income potential that can grow over time, providing financial stability and flexibility for moms seeking to contribute to their household income.

The power of network marketing lies in the trust that individuals have in their personal networks. When a mom becomes a distributor for a product or service, her family and friends are more likely to support her business endeavors. The genuine belief in the products or services being offered, combined with the trust built over the years, makes network marketing an organic extension of the relationships moms already have.

Despite the evident benefits of affiliate and network marketing for moms, these industries often face skepticism and criticism. It's time to dispel the old beliefs surrounding these business models and encourage support for the women in our lives who choose to embark on these entrepreneurial journeys.

Affiliate marketing and network marketing have been subject to various stigmas, often portrayed as pyramid schemes or get-rich-quick schemes. It's essential to distinguish between legitimate business models and fraudulent activities. By educating ourselves and others about the intricacies of these industries, we can overcome the stigmas attached to them and appreciate the genuine opportunities they provide.

As with any business endeavor, due diligence is crucial. Moms considering affiliate or network marketing should thoroughly research the companies they are interested in partnering with. Reputable companies have transparent compensation plans, clear product or service offerings, and a track record of success. By arming themselves with knowledge, moms can make informed decisions and navigate the business landscape with confidence.

It's time to shift the narrative from skepticism to support. Instead of questioning the legitimacy of affiliate and network marketing, let's celebrate the entrepreneurial spirit of moms who choose these paths. By encouraging and supporting mompreneurs, we contribute to the creation of inclusive and empowering environments where women can thrive in their personal and professional lives.

Affiliate and network marketing offer tangible opportunities for moms to achieve financial independence, flexibility, and personal growth. By understanding the unique advantages these business models provide, we can dispel myths, challenge stigmas, and support the women in our lives who choose to embrace these entrepreneurial journeys. It's time to celebrate the diverse paths to success and recognize the power of affiliate and network marketing in empowering moms to create fulfilling and sustainable careers.

Kelli-Sue Miller

B-Epic Worldwide Inc.
Independent Brand Partner & Area Manager - B-Epic Bermuda

www.linkedin.com/in/kelli-sue-miller-994197144
www.facebook.com/kelli.miller3158
https://www.instagram.com/bepicbermudagirl
www.bepic.com//kmiller1970
www.bepicbuilder.com//kmiller1970

Born in Bermuda, I am an only child, Mom of two beautiful daughters Harley 18 & Jordan 14. I love animals, especially horses, pickleball, golf & travelling. I have lived in 2 major cities (London & Boston) & travelled all over the world. I am also a very grateful recovering addict. I have been in Network Marketing for 2 1/2 years in the Health & Wellness Industry, specifically All-Natural Health & Wellness Supplements. Within 6 months, I became a six-figure earning Entrepeneur hitting diamond status, #14 top recruiter in a worldwide multimillion dollar company. Country Area Manager, with a team of 17 Independent Brand Partners. I have helped over a 1000 wonderful people, add more life to their years & become the best version of themselves, improving their overall health and other amazing women make a second income.

MOMS IN NETWORK MARKETING

By Kelli-Sue Miller

When I was asked to be a co-author and contribute to this book alongside a plethora of amazing women, I was speechless and honored. It left me questioning whether my journey and how I found Network Marketing would be worthy of this book and your eyes. Life is all about stepping out of our comfort zone and growing, right? So here goes.

I am a mom of two beautiful daughters, Harley my 18-year-old and Jordan who is 14. They are my absolute world and life. They are what keeps me going and wanting to be a better person, a better woman. I live for them…Literally!! Now, I'm sure most mothers feel the same way about their children; however, when I say I live for them literally, I mean that. You see, I am an addict. A drug addict, to be point blank. An addict in recovery now, after many falls and recoveries. It is my daughters who give me the will, the tenacity, and the perseverance to never give up.

I have battled addiction publicly for 15 years, and it's been a beautiful and tragic journey. I say beautiful because I am a true believer that we go through what we go through to make us who we are today. What doesn't kill us makes us stronger!

After many long years of battling this insidious disease, in and out of treatment centers that didn't work (mainly because I wasn't ready), I experienced probably the worst relapse during the COVID pandemic in 2020. The isolation nearly killed me. I decided then that I would leave Bermuda once again to seek treatment; this time I was desperate and tired. After completing a three-month rehab program, I chose to continue and moved into a Women's Recovery House in South Carolina for 10 months. I was working two, and later three jobs, working 14 hours a day, physically and mentally exhausted. No energy, barely any sleep, and eating to feel better. At the same time, I gained weight like no tomorrow, to the tune of an extra 30 lbs. This affected my self-esteem, self-worth, and how I looked at myself. I thought, "This cannot be what recovery looks like."

Then the day came when my phone rang and it would be the beginning of my life changing for the better. It was a dear friend of mine who knew I was struggling with my weight and well-being. She recommended these all-natural, plant-based supplements. At first, I wasn't interested. I was convinced it was a load of crap. Finally, I got to the point where I just couldn't stand to look at myself in the mirror anymore, so I caved and said OK. Now, at the time, remember I said I was working 14 hours and I was getting paid $4.48 per hour. Ok, you can pick your mouth up off the floor now! I was barely making ends meet, so the idea of parting with $99 to purchase a 30-day supply of the company's #1 combo pack, which my friend assured me would help with energy, gut health, and sleep (including weight loss) seemed crazy, but I said what the heck. Something had to give - either the extra pounds or my wallet. Well, the pounds won.

Those three capsules would change my life; they did more than I could ever imagine. Not only did they improve my overall health within days but I slept like a baby for the first time in 20+ years, and the pounds started melting away to the tune of 30 lbs in five months. It was then that my friend told me about the opportunity within this company to share these products with my friends and family and be paid for it. I immediately said sign me up! That's how much I loved and believed in these products.

At first, I was like, "I don't believe it," "I don't know how to do this," "I will never make a living this way," "What if I fail?" Well, I didn't. I succeeded beyond my expectations and those of everyone else who was skeptical. My biggest supporter in life, my aunt, said, "Don't come home unless you can support yourself." To live comfortably in Bermuda, you need an income of approximately $10k a month. I was able to do that now and she was shocked and pleased. She was now off the hook of paying my bills. She is a saint!

After only four months, I had not only proven to the company that I was a valued member of the company, but they also allowed me to take the product line to Bermuda and become the Area Manager! Completely unheard of! I had my own blinking distribution center in the third richest country in the WORLD. I had no experience in Network Marketing, nor did I have any experience in how to share and market these products on a social media platform. Sure, I had a Facebook page, but up until then it was full of silly memes - I fancy myself a bit of a comedian. I'm told I'm funny. In fact, my dear and beautiful friend Crystal Simmons, who very kindly agreed to proofread my chapter before submitting it (she's an English Major thank goodness), returned it to me with typed in red and capital letters – YOU ARE LOL! Love her, thank you, babes.

I never dreamed what would happen. People on Facebook started noticing my posts, they started listening and relating to my struggles, and they decided to try the product. I think one of the biggest attractions was that they are all-natural, plant-based, available worldwide, and readily available right in Bermuda. I do come from a customer service background (thanks Dad), so I knew that was going to be a key component of our success along with offering free delivery island-wide. I started this business doing deliveries on my bike, rain, blow, or shine. After a year, I bought my company car with cash!!

Well, they were a hit within six months, sales were at an all-time high of $60k a month (keeping in mind Bermuda's population is approx. 65,000). In my capacity as an Independent Brand Partner (IBP) (I wore two hats, Area Manager & IBP) I was making 50% commission, hitting Silver, Gold, and Platinum, building a team of 16 people, and winning three incentives trips thanks to being in the top 50 salespeople worldwide - craaaaazy. When submitting this chapter, I was recognized as the #8 recruiter in my company worldwide - such an honor and accomplishment. As a team, we had approximately 1,500 clients within six months. What set us apart in the B-Epic World was that each client spent more dollar value on each order than anywhere else in the world that B-Epic distributes to. This put us in the top three fastest-growing countries. It was quite honestly unbelievable, and the powers at B-Epic really started to take note of our success.

Network Marketing, and more importantly B-Epic, changed my life. I owe a lot to this company and the Putnam family. They trusted me, believed in me and my ability, and supported me the whole way. I have never found this in a company before to this magnitude.

What was the real clincher was that I was my own boss, finally! A dream come true for me. You see, I also live with ADHD, which was undiagnosed for many years, and thanks to my recovery, I chose not to be medicated. These three capsules have helped me immensely with my ADHD. The freedom to make my schedule and working hours helps immensely. I usually hit a wall after about 45 minutes. So, to be able to stop working, go for a walk, go to the beach, or spend time with my daughters whenever I wanted was an amazing gift.

I have been given the freedom to travel whenever I want because my office literally goes where I go; all I need is my phone and Wi-Fi. It has given me a life beyond my wildest dreams!!

Fast forward to 2023. Sadly, I had another relapse in 2022, and by March 2023, I was done. I was sick and tired of being sick and tired and constantly rebuilding my life after tearing it down every time I was on top. I thought for sure my career with B-Epic was over. Instead, they lovingly said, "Kelli, we value you and love you. Go and get the help you need and hurry back." So, I headed back to the same little town I had gone to before for help, did a 30-day treatment, and I have remained here ever since. When this book is released, I will be celebrating almost 11 months clean, one day at a time - and I still have my business and it's thriving. I'm living in the US, but my business is still thriving in Bermuda, and now growing in the US, Canada, and the UK, all because I can work from anywhere in the world - FREEDOM!!

My priority is my recovery, and this business allows me to do that. I get up at 6 AM, prep for my day, have a recovery meeting at 7:30 AM for an hour, then three hours of work, then another recovery meeting, and then the gym or a walk in nature. I then work for an hour or two in the early evenings. Where else can you find this? I have never found it anywhere else. Who else has it better than me? I don't know but I will tell you this: I am forever grateful to this industry, B-Epic, and my family. My life is Epic today!

Because of this business, I have reconnected with so many old friends and made amazing new friends. Most of my clients are now close friends - my mentor in this company is one of my best friends, along with being my human calculator and therapist. I met people on planes and trains, who have become customers and really good friends, just from talking about my business (some of them being really good looking lol). Without the support of all these people, my dreams would have never come true - I did not do this on my own!

As if my life couldn't get any better, my oldest daughter Harley, who I spoke about above, now works alongside me and runs the Bermuda Distribution Centre whilst I'm here in the US working remotely whilst focusing on my recovery. She handles all the filling of our customer orders, free deliveries island-wide, clearing shipments, and all the storage at 18!!

My message is to any mother who thinks family and a career are impossible, hear it from the horse's mouth, "It is possible and so much more!!!"

Today, I no longer look at myself as just a woman in recovery from addiction. I am an amazing mom, a kickass businesswoman, a six-figure-earner, an entrepreneur, and I'm becoming the "Best Version Of Myself". If I can do it, so can you. Believe in yourself, you're worth it!!!

If no one told you today, I love you. Kelli xx

Cathy Callahan

Maxwell Leadership
Certified Coach, Teacher, Trainer and Speaker

https://www.linkedin.com/in/cathycallahan
www.facebook.com/cathyann0722
www.instagram.com/heysweetmomma
www.pcatu.com
www.pcatu.co

Cathy Callahan, a Midwest mom of boys, values simplicity, fun, and effectiveness in business. Moving from teaching to network marketing to spend more time with family, she brings 17 years of experience in the field. Cathy also managed a family home care business, adding to her diverse skill set. In 2019, she pivoted back to network marketing, embracing online methods. Since 2020, Cathy has been mentoring female entrepreneurs, specializing in virtual events. Her recent achievement is a partnership in the only all-in-one marketing platform for network marketers, unique for its focus on automated Facebook group strategies for growth. Launched in 2023, Cathy's platform is a game-changer for the network marketing industry, embodying her vision of efficient, impactful business solutions.

"HEY SWEET MOMMA": A JOURNEY TO EMPOWERMENT - LESSONS IN MOTHERHOOD, CAREER SHIFTS, AND NETWORK MARKETING SUCCESS

By Cathy Callahan

Hey sweet momma,

Let's take a journey to the day when I was very pregnant with my first child, sitting at the horseshoe table in the back of my kindergarten classroom. It was the first time I experienced the feeling that I may not want to be a teacher anymore. I ALWAYS wanted to be a teacher, except when I thought I wanted to be a nurse (then I found out you don't just take care of newborn babies; you have to draw blood, too).

I wasn't sure what was at the root of this, but I observed a few things all at once that were a testimony that I may have been losing my passion for something I thought I would do forever! I watched my coworkers simply check boxes until they could retire. I couldn't let myself become that way.

I felt a growing disconnection. The passion that once fueled my love for teaching was fading out, and my focus was shifting to my soon-to-be-born first child. After Evan was born, I returned to teaching the following year and was drained. I was giving the best parts of my day to 26 kids that weren't mine, only to come home exhausted with little left for my own. This was the turning point.

Little did I know that network marketing would become the vehicle that not only allowed me to step away from teaching but also set me on an incredible, 17-year journey as a mompreneur. I will show you how to harness the power of change, balance motherhood with entrepreneurship, and navigate the evolving world of network marketing to build a business that is based on purpose, brings you peace and profit, and makes a mass impact. Plus, I will share how you can do this in a fun, simple, and effective way.

Back to that baby: I went back to the full-time classroom after Evan was born. I juggled two jobs alongside teaching to save up for a year's maternity leave when Evan was one and a half years old. During this break, I received a spa party invitation from my friend Angie who was also a room parent in my classroom.

There I met Kim, the representative sharing the products and business information at the event. Kim would eventually become my upline and one of my closest friends. Listening to her share her story, I began to see that maybe I had options I didn't know about before!

In October 2006, I launched my business. I didn't have social media or even texting capabilities. I had to open my wedding guest list and the school buzzbook and make phone calls! My network extended a little beyond my sister, cousin, and a couple of close friends. I have often heard that your clients will become your friends before your friends will become your clients. And that is ok!

I had plenty of people who didn't get why I would want to do a business like this, and hosting spa parties and emptying guests' dirty foot buckets wasn't a draw for everyone like it was for me.

I worked the system, and six months later, I was able to resign from my teaching career. I fully embraced motherhood and network marketing. It was an incredible journey filled with ups and downs as well as memorable, sometimes unpredictable, moments.

There were plenty of laughs and also tears. There were evenings of cancellations, no-shows, and no sales. There were also nights where customers turned into friends and guests evolved into team members.

These experiences were so different from my teaching days. It hit me when I sat back and thought about the $25 Walmart gift card I got at Christmas one year as a teacher. At that time, that was a big deal. I found that network marketing offered tangible incentives for hard work like I had never experienced before. From taking my sister on two trips and my son to Atlantis in the Bahamas, to earning Tiffany's jewelry, car bonuses, and more - the rewards were a testament to the effort I put in.

In 2011, I reached a VP rank, which was in the top 2% of the company. My initial goal was achieved by simply replacing my teaching income and being home each day to walk Evan to school, volunteer in his classroom, and be the PTO mom and president I wanted to be at that time. However, I had this friend and neighbor named Dave, and one day he drove by my house as I was outside washing my red Toyota Camry and he asked, "So when are ya getting that Benz?"

For some reason, I said, "Give me three months." WHAT?? Wait, what? What was I thinking? Inside I went to draw circle charts and map out 32,000 in sales. I saw big holes in that piece of paper, and I decided to buckle down and get to work. Achieving VP was significant because along with my sales, I also built a team of dreamers and doers.

Along with that rank came a fun celebration. My parents sat in the front row, and I could see how proud they were of me. This mattered a lot because telling my mother I wanted to leave teaching was one of the hardest conversations I have had in my life.

But it was only one year into that leave that she said, "You have become a different person. You did the right thing." I was no longer the super shy, insecure girl that stood against the wall. To grow my business, I had to grow myself and focus outside of my needs. It changed who I was and set me up for all of what would come.

Weathering Life's Storms

In 2012, a phone call on Valentine's Day dramatically shifted the course of my life. My mother, who was visiting my sister in Tennessee, called from the ER. I remember vividly that she had been given nine days left to live. Defying the initial diagnosis, she lived for nine more months. It was a testimony of this industry that I didn't have to ask for time off.

A month before her passing, I found myself considering a departure from network marketing to take over the family business. When I opened up to my mom, she said, "Catherine, you have never wanted to do my business."

And she was right, I never had until then. I felt an unfamiliar conviction within me. I responded with, "I think I can do it. I think I can apply a lot of what I have learned, and I would have some of the same flexibility and freedom, too."

After she passed, I stepped back from MLM and stepped into an unknown territory. My decision wasn't about the allure of senior home care over the spa parties, despite their sometimes humorous mishaps. Rather, it was deeply rooted in personal experience.

I recalled my mother's final days, the assistance she required, and the relief our family desperately needed during that period. I gained an appreciation and a unique perspective on the senior care industry.

Embracing Growth: Lessons from MLM to Senior Care

The journey of growth within the senior care industry was beyond anything I could have imagined. Drawing from my MLM experience, I approached the business with the same people-focused service and strategic business mindset. I set growth goals by breaking them down into bite-sized pieces, created an action plan, tracked progress, and repeated the strategies that proved effective.

Note: This is what we must do in any business, and I first learned it in MLM. Ironically, many businesses and most of the MLM industry still don't teach this.

Through the transition, I took on debt to keep the business open. I didn't have pens, flyers, or any typical promotional swag to offer. My business experience, up until that point, was primarily in MLM, involving two or three pamper parties per week. But, this didn't stop me from showing up to the senior vendor events. Instead, I brought along my hand lotion from the pamper parties and offered seniors to have a seat and get a hand massage. I learned to connect with people, and this was one way to stop traffic and get them to engage in meaningful conversations.

Note: You must stop the traffic and get them to engage with you, too! Many marketers today thrive on vanity metrics like views, but that would be like bragging that 300 people came to the vendor fair. How many stopped and talked, though? Do you have a good way to capture traffic? Prepare to invest and grow by giving your time and sincere investment in people.

Growth and New Beginnings: From Business Success to Embracing Motherhood

We experienced remarkable growth in the company. What initially began with just two of us committed to its rebuilding – a special shout-out to Rachel for embarking on this journey with me – eventually expanded. Our team grew to include four office staff and over 50 employees. By my last full year as the owner, we had nearly reached $1 million in revenue. But alongside this business growth, there was another significant development in my life – my family was growing too. During these years, I was blessed with two more boys. I found myself balancing breastfeeding and diaper changes with 24/7 phone calls and caregiver and client concerns.

Lesson: Choose your hand.

2017 marked yet another pivotal turn in my life. I made the heartfelt decision to sell the home care agency. My family supported me, while some of the clients and caregivers did not understand.

> **Lesson:** Not everyone will support you, but you know what you need to do.

The Digital Revolution in Network Marketing: Embracing Change with a Personal Twist

In 2019, I made a return to network marketing, but this time, with a twist. I told my upline I was coming back, but I was not going to do home parties. I had to find a way to work from my closet (for real). After one month of attempting to implement the systems that most of the teams were using, I found myself spinning my wheels, balancing too many things all at once. I couldn't do any more three-way calls, and learning social media and messaging people meant I felt controlled by the DMs.

I decided to take what I knew worked offline, and I went online with virtual parties. Along with that, I sought outside training and marketing classes.

> **Lesson:** You do not have to do things the way everyone else is. If it doesn't resonate, go find a way that does. Follow your heart. You are the one that has to wake up and do the darn thing. Be fired up about it.

And fired up I was. I LOVED doing virtual events. Over the first three months, I was able to rebuild and it took me six months in person to achieve it. I dialed in my processes and I started putting together my steps into a systematic process my team could follow. However, all the resources in the world did not equal a step-by-step process that took the guesswork out and provided a proven framework for them to follow.

> **Lesson**: If you want to team build, have a *KISS*. Keep it Simple System. Teach it, and allow your team to do it differently if they want to. (Independent Rep, not employee, remember?)

I found solace in my closet, and I turned my virtual events into experiences that people loved! I streamlined my processes even more into a once-a-week Evergreen party system, and one week before the pandemic of 2020 hit, I launched this enhanced party process with my team.

Blending business and motherhood was possible in a way like never before. I was able to rebuild a business online twice as quickly as before, and have reached well outside of where I could drive. My mind was blown. I kept learning, sharing, and doing.

The Evolution of an Industry

The next four years were a whirlwind of being a mompreneur and being a part of a vastly changing industry. I had doors open for me when I was willing to share what I was doing with others who were struggling in the online space. I created my first live challenge and course, and they allowed the teacher in me to thrive!

I worked through the variety of needs and challenges that came with being a mom to a teen and littles all at once. I navigated relationship changes, ADHD diagnoses (me and my son), family crises, and plenty of joyful and incredible moments in motherhood and business.

And I witnessed a pivotal shift in network marketing. I have watched social media change the game. I have seen companies close, reps leave, new companies start, and mompreneurs rule this space, using social media and modern-day marketing to accomplish things they never could before.

Through the last 17 years in this industry, I have had one door closed and the next door open. Most recently, I joined the Maxwell Leadership Certified Team and I also co-founded PCATU Social CRM, an extension of my 'Purpose Creator Action Taker University business programs and courses'. It came out of the need we saw in the network marketing and affiliate marketing space for marketing and automation software made for the everyday marketer. We provide the tools strategies and software needed in this new digital landscape for an industry that is still struggling to adapt.

A Journey of Growth and Empowerment

Reflecting on my path, from the early days in the classroom to now coaching as a Maxwell Certified Team Member and a software partner, I can stand above it all and see a journey defined by growth, resilience, and the power of embracing change. I credit so much of who I am, what I know, and how I love people to what I learned in network marketing. I have had the privilege of working with thousands of female entrepreneurs over the last few years. My mission is to empower women with the vision and passion they need to take charge and create a purposeful, profitable, and peaceful business, one that allows you to play all out, even when life happens.

Together, sweet momma, let's continue to navigate the evolving world of network marketing, affiliate marketing, and digital marketing. We're not just building businesses; we're creating legacies of strength, joy, and inspiration for ourselves and our children.

Moving Forward: 2024 and Beyond in Network Marketing

As we step into 2024 and beyond, we know that the industry is changing. No, it has changed. And we must adapt. This change brings both challenges and opportunities, reshaping the way we, as entrepreneurs and especially as women, engage with this evolving business model.

Uniting for a Common Goal

As mothers, businesswomen, thinkers, and innovators, we can rise and continue to propel this incredible industry forward. It's about speaking truths, empowering rather than controlling, and surrounding each other with the knowledge and strength needed to become the best version of ourselves as women, mothers, and entrepreneurs.

As you embrace your journey, I want to leave you with a few things that might simplify and accelerate the path for you and for those you impact:

- **Embrace Modern Marketing, But Never Forget the Foundation**: The heart of our business is connection. As you explore the latest in digital marketing, never lose sight of the foundational principles that got us here: trust, authenticity, and personal relationships. Tell your story. Be open, vulnerable, and honest, always offering hope and inspiration.

- **Automate the Mundane, Personalize What Counts**: There's only so much time between school runs and bedtime stories. Use technology to handle routine tasks and automate repetitive processes. Put your heart into what you do and always provide people with an experience and a transformation over information and facts. Never automate empathy and genuine connections.

- **Keep It Simple, Fun, and Effective**: Juggling family meals, bedtime stories, and your business requires grace and creativity. Simplify your business processes, always make fun and memorable, and let your authentic joy shine (even if it doesn't like everyone else). Stay focused on strategies that bring results and be ready to adapt and evolve.

So hey, sweet momma, can you find the balance (or the blend) between your family and your professional dreams? Is it your season for personal growth and change? Will network or affiliate marketing become part of your story? This journey is about creating businesses with purpose, fostering peace at home, and generating profitable outcomes with a widespread impact.

As we embrace change, leverage modern-day marketing strategies and tools, and maintain genuine connections, I believe we can build businesses like never before. That old saying "in the nooks and crannies" might have some validity with proven systems and technology on our side. With the courage to blend motherhood with entrepreneurship, let's continue to navigate the evolving landscape of network marketing. Here's to our growth, empowerment, and impact in 2024 and beyond! Whether network marketing is a home, a starting point, or a stepping stone to the next big adventure, commit to making a difference.

You've got this!

Cathy

Jennifer Kirkner

Plexus
Brand ambassador

https://www.facebook.com/profile.php?id=100008050218831
https://www.instagram.com/jenniferkirkner/
http://mysite.plexusworldwide.com/jenniferkirknerplexus
Ambassador #902052037

Jennifer Kirkner was born, raised and still resides in the Reading, PA area. She is a sister to James, Liz and Deb Richard. She is married for 5 years to Lenny Kirkner IV. She has 2 daughters Chloe Ohlinger, 22 and Iris Kirkner, 4.

She currently is a stay at home mom, works as a child care provider and has a social marketing position as an independent Plexus Brand Ambassador. She attends Cocalico Community Church in Reinholds, PA.

In her spare time she likes to do fun things with her family, attends church functions, volunteers in children's ministries, connects with friends, reads, listens to worship music and enjoy spending time outside in nature, swimming, attending concerts and live sporting events, traveling to any beach or warm weather for family vacations.

MOM ON TOP!

By Jennifer Kirkner

This is my story of The Mom on top. It's about resilience, hope, and overcoming life situations that I went through. I want to share my story to inspire others to find balance in their lives. I want to share to let others know they are not alone in this. We all have obstacles in life that we must want to improve despite having them. There was no choice of abandonment from my mother regardless of my insecurity in myself due to mental health, loss of loved ones, and a chronic pain illness. That can sure put you down, but we have to always get back up on top. My personal "on top" is my relationship with Jesus, staying faithful to what he wants for me. The most important tool in parenthood is faith in God.

God is the hope when things aren't always good and when situations are still in progress. Faith that he will make it good. We moms want to control everything. Everything was on His timeline, not mine. The ability for most to give up control and need a savior is hard to grasp for most. For example, faith for when your kids aren't kids anymore, having to make their own decisions. Putting them in God's hands in surrender is not as easy as when they were under your roof. Letting go when you used to care for them with your all is hard. To trust in God feels different for you and might be different for them. In exploring life, you are a cheerleader to the great things and the shoulder for them when things don't go their way. You are the guide to start, hoping they will be a light to others, never growing weary of doing good and choosing joy in all situations. God's way, not our own.

I encourage you that you can overcome anything if you are willing to have faith in more than your own strength, hope that things will be better, and make changes to align with that. If it isn't working for you, change it. Find a balance that works for you, especially as a working mom.

My bond with my older daughter, Chloe, is so great. We share and talk about everything. I have given her so much advice, little by little, over the years and I can tell she listened. Mostly concerning that, we can make decisions, but they all have consequences. Good or bad. The advice that we have to live with them and the sum of our decisions makes up our life. She made her choices and I was cheering her on all the way. She wants to make me proud. She wants to make her situation better. She finds the way. I feel like my life is an example of this too. This is a result of the time, attention, and encouragement I put into her. I am so grateful for our relationship. I am excited to see what her future will become. She has a drive in her. I see in her what I was at her age, digging deep to get to better situations.

This past year we celebrated in Las Vegas for her 21st and my 40th birthdays! We always wanted to do that, and I am so glad that we had an experience like that together. We always traveled together around her birthday to explore new places. After graduating this year, Chloe is moving to Charlotte, North Carolina to pursue a career in business full time with a company.

I was raised by a Dad of four, I was the youngest of three girls and one boy. Since I was two, my parents were divorced. My Dad raised us alone. Looking back and thinking of his situation is so inspiring to me. He truly showed he loved us through his humor, Godly teachings, regular meals at the table, and fun car rides with oldies playing and singing along. He had a great work ethic that all my siblings and I inherited. He was an electrician, usually working early mornings to early evenings, 12-hour days. He was always cheerful and happy. We attended church my whole life. We spent Sundays and Wednesdays at church. He served in the church as a Bible study teacher for Sunday school and in our home weekly. At the church that we attended for many years is where he met his wife, my Stepmom. They were married when I was 13. Shortly into the marriage, she was diagnosed with Fibromyalgia, a chronic pain illness. She rested all the time. She gave up her factory job she had for many years because it was too hard on her body. At the time I knew nothing of the illness before her having it, so I didn't understand. Unfortunately, when I was 19, only six years into their marriage, my Dad passed away from cancer. Having home hospice care and my stepmother caring for him, he passed peacefully in the home that I was raised in my whole life. Going through this was so hard, especially being a new parent myself at a young age.

I had to step up and figure it out. My dad's life inspired me to be the best mom I could be.

Becoming a mom and not having a mother in my life growing up was often a challenge making me wonder, "Can I do this?"

I pursued the workforce right after high school. It didn't start there, though. I had past jobs as a newspaper route carrier at the age of eight that was shared with three of my older siblings. At the age of 14, I started working at an hourly rate. Gaining restaurant experience and retail management skills along the way made me who I am today. The official first promotion to management originally came at the age of 19.

I was married to Chloe's dad for 10 years. We divorced when Chloe was 10 years old. Chloe chose to stay in the house she grew up in with her dad for the first two years. We had the custody agreement for her choice because of her age. I lived in an apartment close by. This was one of the hardest times I had to go through, especially the nights of not having her with me. Being alone during that time was the worst. This was a time when I had to pray relentlessly and fully trust God. I filled my alone time with Bible study participation in a small group from church, serving in the Children's Ministry, Fellowship

Committee, and Missions. Thankfully, Chloe then decided to stay with only me at the beginning of her teenage years. As a divorced mom, it was difficult to take care of her and work full-time alone. During this time, I put most of my efforts into work, doing my best to be there for Chloe. I can say my goal was to show up for her when she needed me.

I have been married for five years now. Chloe was my maid of honor. Starting my life over again was not an easy decision for me. I came so far in my career, and balance of life, especially in financial giving and serving in the church. Giving my time to someone else other than my child in pursuing a relationship with my husband was difficult. I decided to start all over again for the love of the relationship I had with Chloe. Why wouldn't I want to do it again!? It was the time I had to pray for strength every day, all day. At Chloe's high school graduation, I was pregnant with my second daughter, Iris. We decided my husband would be a stay-at-home dad. We both had careers leading up to her birth. We planned to do daycare, but when COVID started, we changed our plan to keep her home.

After graduating in June, Chloe moved the day after her 18th birthday in July to Philadelphia, PA, which is an hour and a half away from where I live. She has been pursuing a Business Degree at the Community College of Philadelphia and works at her college as well. She serves in student government. At the of age 19, Chloe started her own cosmetic business, Pesos Cosmetics. She started all on her own, with zero help from her mom. Chloe promotes her business through her social media and her following of friends. She consistently kept it all going like it was nothing. She was able to pursue so many avenues like modeling, writing, and creating. Building her brand on social media was unbelievably inspiring to me. She took her talents, advice, and book reviews to her audience and built a confidence in herself that I never had. She took a risk with nothing to lose.

She inspired me in a way that taking risks can lead you to great things.

Taking a leap. Start somewhere. Go for the promotion. This is a mantra that gave me hope. A hope that if you want to do a career you love, do that.

I really did enjoy going right into the workforce. I worked through many promotions and received many blessings from my work in the restaurant management industry. My most recent position in the industry provided well for my family but did not offer my work/life balance when becoming a mom to my second child. As a working mom, work shoves its way to being a priority. I learned at this time that being dependent on God is how I can put things in perspective. How is this all going to work out? After being in the restaurant management industry for 20 years, where would I be my career for the next 20 years if I had a choice? My plans did not work out.

I was with that company for eight years when I was diagnosed with Fibromyalgia, a widespread chronic pain illness. I knew some but not all of the challenges I had to face. I spent the early part of 2022 on a medical leave of absence from work. I was waiting to get a medical procedure that would provide relief for four weeks. My life completely changed within a year of being diagnosed with my illness. The loss of my career seemed like a loss of identity. Asking God, "Who am I?" I was lost-I was used to working for all these years. This was unlike me to not be working. By the end of 2022, I was not able to work. My doctor did not fill out my return to work form due to my condition. It had gotten that much worse in that little amount of time.

Immediately I sought counseling to transition from one life to another. How would I make a living? Going through so many sceneries in my head, I had to logically think about what to do. Physically, mentally, and emotionally. A job that I could do from home. When you have to accommodate your physical needs, you have to picture doing things. My body reacts badly to sitting or standing too long. I can't lift or I'll pay for it the next day through pain. Stress is a deal breaker for me. Stress gives me terrible anxiety attacks. Also, if I get sick, it takes a while for me to recover. Unfortunately, I can say there is not a day that goes by that I'm not in pain.

I needed a solution to my health and income for my household. I tried Plexus for gut health in 2020 then gave up. I remembered feeling better when taking the all-natural supplements. I decided to start my health journey again but with intentions other than losing weight. I needed the ability to feel better daily and find a career I could do from home with my daughter for me to care for full-time now. Network marketing with Plexus was a game-changer for me. I could run my own business from home.

As of now, I am a stay-at-home mom to my daughter, I work as a nanny, and run my independent Plexus business. This is so fulfilling as a mom, to balance family and work life. This is a role that is new to me. I have always been in the workforce and transitioned to choosing family too. Being out of the house as a mother doesn't mean you ever stop being one. Your family is your first thought and greatest motivation. Take time to enjoy the moments when you get them, if you get them.

When my husband transitioned back to work after two years of being home, it was a hard transition. We got used to the routine. We completely swapped roles as I couldn't return to work after having a medical leave. My illness took away a career I thought I wanted, putting me in a position to get well and achieve my personal business goals instead. I'm very thankful for this option when disability could have been my near future. I find this career path fulfills my financial goals and aligns with my values. I look forward to continued success in my journey and the ability to help others overcome their battle over the challenge of health.

I chose Plexus because I saw a community of women who overcame health issues similar to my own and with shared spiritual beliefs. They care to share their journey and want to help others. Helping women with their health is important to me because I am a woman who has a lot of health issues due to chronic illness. I don't want to take prescribed medications that have long-term effects on my body. These are all-natural supplements to support gut health, weight management, an active lifestyle, and skin care. This has helped me so much with my Fibromyalgia symptoms such as brain fog, fatigue, depression, mood swings, anxiety, panic attacks, sleep quality, IBS, restless legs, joint pain, stiffness, Costochondritis, Electric-like nerve pain throughout the body, and inflammation.

My hope by sharing my story is to help others change their life for the better. As a Christian, I regularly reflect on my life. I asked God, "Why do I have this pain? What is the purpose, Lord?" I believe when you go through something new, you have to take time to adjust your living. There is no cure. Yet. You have to live with the pain. Find a way. Then share with others. I believe I have this illness for me to help others try to live their best life despite this illness. The pain is not going to go away if you don't do anything about it. My priority from now on is my health. I had to take action on preventative care, celebrate all the big and small victories, be the best version of myself for my family and business as well, and help others along the way.

Leslie Lahd

Bravenly Global
Senior Director

https://www.linkedin.com/in/leslie-lahd-875510160/
https://www.facebook.com/LeslieLLahdBusiness
https://www.instagram.com/50isnotanfword_leslielahd/
https://leslielahd.bravenlyglobal.com/

After nearly three decades in the corporate sector, I faced a turning point. Confronted with continuous cutbacks and increasing stress, I departed from my career to dedicate myself to my direct sales business. This transition was more than a career move; it was a necessity, especially with limited job prospects and a diagnosis of advanced ulcerative colitis and other autoimmune issues. I needed to prioritize my health, and my 'side gig' provided the required flexibility to balance work and well-being.

Now, six years later, I've partnered with a wellness company, embracing life at 50 and beyond with newfound vigor. I'm healthier than ever and have developed a passion for helping other women achieve the same lifestyle. My days are richly filled with managing my business, golfing or traveling with my husband, spending quality time with our kids, family, and friends, and embracing life's adventures.

REDEFINING RETIREMENT: AN ENCORE CAREER AFTER KIDS, CORPORATE, AND 50

By Leslie Lahd

Ever had one of those 'aha' moments at the most unexpected times? For me, it happened when I was squished in an airplane seat, coming back from my very first conference. There I sat, trying to figure out how to keep this excitement once the plane landed and I was back to my real life. I knew I was done – done with the corporate grind - and I needed to tell my husband. At 49, with nearly 30 years in the same industry, I sketched out a plan on my notepad to show him why I needed to dive headfirst into my direct sales business. Sounds crazy, right? But that's where my journey took a complete U-turn, and I swapped boardrooms and whiteboards for kitchens and product demos. I had to be 'convinced' to attend this conference, so how could I ever have anticipated it would be the catalyst for an entire career change??

I still remember when I first became a consultant; I had no idea what it meant, or what opportunities it could provide. All I wanted were my beloved products conveniently delivered to my post box, so imagine my excitement when I found out I could get them at a discount!!! It was like I had just hit the jackpot! I didn't know anything about the opportunity to earn income, nor did I have the desire to learn more.

I already had a very stressful and demanding career. I also had a home business that I was building from scratch, my husband has a small trucking company, and we had a cattle farm – what I didn't need was something else to do! So, when my upline sent a friend request and reached out by email, I ignored her for a bit, but eventually, my sense of business etiquette won over and I responded. As I explained to her how I had no intention of this being anything more than me utilizing the consultant discount, she kindly asked if I would at least be open to having a launch party. I really had no idea what this entailed, but said yes, knowing that I already had a friend who wanted to host a party once she found out about my new venture. She loved the products too and volunteered at the first opportunity.

What I didn't expect was to have such a good time and love it so much! What a fun evening; we sampled the products, had a little wine, a lot of laughs, and I even booked three more parties. Then, the following Friday, $162 showed up in my bank account – wait, what, you can earn money too??? Seriously, that's how disconnected I was!

I was gaining momentum and not only was I growing a business hanging out in people's kitchens, but I was thoroughly enjoying it and even now fondly reflect on the first time I earned a bonus. It was 3% of my sales that month, so about $65, and let me tell you that was one of my proudest moments in business! So weird because I had earned a lot of bonuses and gifts in my years on the corporate ladder that were worth much more than that, but for some yet-to-be-discovered reason, this meant so much more.

I was on a roll and even earned a 'Hot Shot' award from my upline which included a free pass to our upcoming conference. This was where everything changed for me, and I would compose that exit strategy letter on the plane ride home.

Within a year, I would go on to earn the company incentive trip as a consultant, which was pretty rare. I would travel to various locations in Canada and the USA for company events. I would meet the most wonderful people, many of whom are friends to this day. I'd continue to grow a thriving business, even hosting online events from a cruise ship in the Mediterranean, and would be diagnosed with advanced ulcerative colitis and auto-immune arthritis and be scheduled for a hysterectomy – my world blew up!

The diagnosis was a wake-up call. I had to make some big changes, including an aggressive treatment plan to manage my health. Dealing with the constant fatigue, pain, and mobility issues in my shoulders, hands, and hips was a daily battle. I would often "joke" that my day had to happen between 10 am and 2 pm because before then, I was sitting with a heating pad in the sauna or stretching, just to get my body moving. After, I was likely on the couch, exhausted from whatever I had to do that day! If events were on the calendar, I would literally have to rest up for a couple of days to be prepared and not schedule anything for a day or two after so I could recover. This was a very difficult period for me. It wasn't just my body that was struggling either. Mentally, I was in a rough spot. I felt down a lot, kind of like being stuck in a funk I couldn't shake off. This wasn't the life I wanted to live, but fortunately, I did have my business, and it was like a little ray of light. It was something I could do even from bed or the couch, and it gave me this sense of purpose when pretty much everything else was just too much. I started to appreciate the whole direct sales thing. It let me work in my own way, at my own pace, sometimes from a doctor's office or the parking lot outside while I waited for appointments. That flexibility was a game-changer for me. Life was throwing me some curveballs but somehow it was all made a little easier knowing I still had something worthwhile to do and was contributing to our household.

Not long after, something with my business didn't feel right and I found myself more and more uninterested, frustrated, feeling alone, unaccomplished, and without passion or purpose! Even though my business grew and thrived through 2020 and all its pitfalls, it was a very stressful time, and of no one thing, event, or any person's fault, things changed for me.

I was no longer aligned with my company. I still loved the product; I still loved the people I worked with, had a huge appreciation for my customers, and massive respect for the company. I really, really tried to make it work, but something was off.

During this time, I saw a Facebook ad for a three-day virtual party course and thought maybe this was the key. Not knowing how I would feel any given day or how much energy I would have to give, I found it more and more difficult to get back to in-person parties. I couldn't give my best or my all and this was hard for me, so maybe mastering online parties was the key!

Well, it definitely helped. I really enjoyed what I learned. I benefited from the results of applying various techniques but something was still missing, and I couldn't put my finger on it. I was so grateful for a business I could do from home, during hours that worked for me and gave me the flexibility to look after myself first, so it didn't make a lot of sense - but I still felt off!

The virtual event was my first experience with business coaching from an external source and I enjoyed it very much. I decided I would look into what else they had to offer, liked what I saw, and came to the realization that if my business was going to survive, it needed to be invested in.

I signed up for coaching, and with that, I did a deep dive into how I was doing business, whether it was working for me or against me, what was it I really wanted, and finding out if my business could support that. So many questions needed to be answered and what I discovered from it all: I felt like a fraud! I was portraying a message socially that I wasn't living in real life. What my company promoted and stood for was not how I was doing life nor could I completely relate to it any longer. Not in a bad way, just a different way.

My life was now about to get better! Increased trips to see my medical team combined with a holistic approach to healing that involved visits to my naturopath, acupuncturist, stretch therapist, and massage therapist – all of whom kept me moving and helped with my mobility issues. My diet also needed a drastic overhaul as I found out I was highly intolerant to eggs, dairy, and corn (plus a few other items where there was an intolerance but not as severe). My wellness became my every day and involved a need for healing a very damaged gut.

In the summer of 2022, a friend shared something she was using an all-natural, naturopath-formulated product. She sent me a sample that sat on my counter for another month or so until one afternoon I decided to give it a try. I didn't even notice until about 4 pm that afternoon that I wasn't on the couch; instead, I was getting things done. I couldn't tell you the last time I had afternoon energy. It was so foreign but exciting!

I was already on a bunch of supplements my naturopath recommended, but the sustained energy I got this time was something else, something I hadn't felt in ages. That got me curious. I'm an analyst at heart, and so, I started digging into these products, the company behind them, and even the people who started it all. And the more I learned, the more it felt right. When the chance came to join this company, I didn't just step in – I leaped.

It was like everything clicked into place. Here was a business that wasn't just about selling stuff; it was about the kind of healing journey I was on – focusing on nutrition, top-notch ingredients, and stuff that's good for gut health. And the best part? I could share this journey and help others like me who needed these products. It was more than just a job; it was a mission that lined up perfectly with my own path to getting better.

I love that I have the flexibility to focus on my health and take time to look after myself when needed! I feel better, look better, and have more energy and joy than I've had in a long time. My business is thriving and growing, I get to help others every single day with their wellness and/or business journeys, and this all happened in about 10 months – this is what passion and purpose will do!

Looking back, I realize how my initial skepticism about direct sales mirrored a common stereotype. But this journey has taught me about the power of open-mindedness and embracing change. It's not just about selling products; it's about building connections, growing personally, and finding unexpected joy in new beginnings. It's about friendships and growth and pride and doing something for you and your family. It's about supporting each other and lifting people up. It's about meeting lifelong friends you never knew you had, learning about yourself, and growing as a person. It is an investment - an investment of your time, your energy, your heart, and your money. But what you put into it comes back to YOU, often multiplied, and that's pretty special!

Now, my days are mine to design. They're filled with personal growth, self-care, and time spent exactly where it feels right. I'm surrounded by incredible women, each crafting their own dreams and making a real difference for their families. And the best part? I'm right there with them, mentoring and learning all at the same time.

The flexibility of what this life offers is something I dreamt of. I can grab lunch on a whim, have my little nieces come by whenever they like, drop in to see my folks, hit the golf course, take a day trip to discover something new, or jump on a jet or a cruise ship whenever the whim strikes. Along the way, I've crossed paths with some amazing folks and discovered so much about myself – about who I am and who I aspire to be. And guess what? I'm doing all this at 55, with absolutely no plans of slowing down.

Looking ahead, there's even more excitement on the horizon. My husband's retirement is just a couple of years away, and we've got big plans. We're going to dive into this endeavor together. I'm full of anticipation for a future absolutely full of adventures, a purpose-driven life, a healthy lifestyle that syncs up with my business, the sheer joy of helping others on their journeys, and, of course, savoring all the things we love.

It's been an incredible honor to share my journey on these pages alongside so many inspiring women and I'm so grateful I could be a part of this. I hope to light a spark in someone out there, to show that excitement and opportunity don't have an expiry date. It's never too late to embrace a new beginning! You've got a wealth of experiences, a lifetime of growth, and it'd be such a waste not to put that to use. Remember, direct sales doesn't care about age; it welcomes everyone with open arms. So, to all the moms navigating any new phase of life, but especially those filling the space between the kids leaving the nest and the golden years of retirement, there just might be a world of passion and purpose waiting for you. Bet on yourself. Don't sell yourself short. Find that thing that sets your soul on fire and dive in. Life is an adventure waiting to be lived – go out there and claim yours!

Gina Redzanic

CEO of Gina Redzanic, Inc.

https://www.facebook.com/gina.pantanoredzanic
https://www.instagram.com/the.self.confidence.coach
www.ginaredzanic.com

Gina Redzanic is a certified Business and Success Coach, published author, and income strategist. Gina is happily married raising two daughters in North Carolina. She balances motherhood and her career through discipline and self-motivation, a practice she teaches her clients.

Gina initially dove into entrepreneurship in 2008, when she and her husband started their own fitness business from the trunk of their car! She went on to build her own 7-figure organization in network marketing and continued to commit herself to continued education in personal and business development.

She has been featured in many publications like Yahoo! Finance, Brainz Magazine, and was named Top 10 Leadership Coaches in Influencive magazine. Gina specializes in helping her clients build their brand, their self- confidence and their income.

UNLOCK YOUR PERSONAL BRAND

By Gina Redzanic

The benefits of creating a relevant business in affiliate or network marketing for moms are typically based upon the fact that, as moms, we can be present with our children while earning an income that comes with time flexibility. The hard work and grit of the building phase are worth it when you know the result will be time freedom. Working moms usually battle with missing out on milestones, field trips, and sick days with their children. On the flip side, stay-at-home moms often crave their own success and earnings. This is where building a business in affiliate or network marketing has huge advantages.

Personal Success

For over a decade now I have been an entrepreneur. While I have had success with a brick-and-mortar business with my husband, as a solopreneur I have reached incredible recognition and income in the industry of network marketing. I assumed once I was a mother that I'd be fulfilled as a stay-at-home mom, but I quickly realized that there was also a desire in me to achieve business success of my own. I am a great example of someone who wants to be a full-time mom but who wants to achieve financial and business success as well. In 2013 I was introduced to network marketing with a heath and wellness company. That introduction changed my life. For starters, the ability to earn income from home was exactly what I craved. However, the journey became so much more than the financial achievements. Personal development throughout my journey was a huge advantage to my growth as a leader and businesswoman. This industry provided incredible insight. I achieved success both financially and through many achievements in leadership. I built a seven-figure organization in less than eight years. I discovered strengths and passions I didn't realize I had! The greatest attribute for me has truly been that my two daughters have not only witnessed my business growth and personal achievements but have also been a part of it. They have been able to see their mom as a successful businesswoman AND a present mother.

Getting to Know the Industry

Before you dive into this industry, it is important to know the different genres available to create your success. Network marketing, affiliate marketing, social selling, and direct sales are all distinct approaches to distributing products or services, but they differ significantly in their structure, methods, and relationships between the seller and the consumer.

Network Marketing: Network marketing, often referred to as multi-level marketing (MLM), is a business model that relies on a network of distributors or representatives who not only sell products or services but also recruit and train others to do the same. Individuals involved in network marketing typically earn commissions from their direct sales as well as from the sales made by the distributors they've recruited. This creates a multi-tiered, compensation structure where earnings can stem from both personal sales and the sales generated by their downline or team.

Affiliate Marketing: Affiliate marketing is a performance-based marketing strategy where individuals or affiliates promote products or services offered by a company through unique tracking links or codes. Affiliates earn a commission for each sale, lead, or action generated through their promotional efforts. Unlike network marketing, affiliate marketers do not recruit a team or build a downline. Their focus is primarily on driving traffic and conversions through their promotional channels such as websites, blogs, social media, or email lists.

Social Selling: Social selling involves using social media platforms as a primary tool for selling products or services. It emphasizes building relationships, engaging with potential customers, and leveraging social networks to drive sales. Social sellers often provide valuable content, product demonstrations, and personalized interactions to create a more engaging and authentic buying experience. While similar to network marketing in terms of building relationships, social selling typically does not involve recruiting a team or creating a multi-level structure for earnings.

Direct Sales: Direct sales involve selling products or services directly to consumers without the need for a physical retail location. It often includes one-on-one demonstrations, home parties, or online sales where representatives showcase and sell products directly to customers. Unlike network marketing, direct sales usually do not involve building a team or recruiting others. Representatives in direct sales earn commissions solely based on their individual sales efforts.

In summary, while network marketing, affiliate marketing, social selling, and direct sales all involve selling products or services, they differ in their compensation structures, recruitment aspects, and the primary focus of the sales efforts. Network marketing involves building a team and earning from both personal sales and team sales, affiliate marketing focuses on promoting products for commission, social selling emphasizes leveraging social media for sales, and direct sales involves individual sales efforts without building a team.

Key Elements of a Personal Brand:

To reach "side hustle" success is not very difficult in this industry, but to truly harness all the potential this industry offers, you need to go "all in," and you also need to stand out. Most people struggle with this. They don't understand or know how to brand themselves. It takes time, patience, and a lot of focus, but it is necessary if you have a goal to make it to the top and also have longevity in this industry.

In the current landscape of professional and personal growth, the concept of personal branding has emerged as a pivotal tool for success. Your personal brand is not merely a logo or a tagline; it is the unique combination of your skills, values, experiences, and reputation that sets you apart from others. But first, let's dive into the details of defining and cultivating a compelling personal brand.

It involves intentional self-promotion, but more importantly, it focuses on authenticity, consistency, and the value you offer to your audience or network.

1. Self-Discovery and Authenticity: Start by understanding yourself - your strengths, passions, and what makes you unique. Authenticity is the cornerstone of personal branding. Be genuine, honest, and true to yourself. Your brand should reflect your authentic self, aligning with your beliefs and values.

2. Identifying Your Unique Value Proposition: What sets you apart from others? Define your unique skills, expertise, and the specific value you bring to the table. It could be your problem-solving abilities, your creative approach, or your exceptional communication skills. Highlight these strengths to differentiate yourself.

3. Consistency Across Platforms: Consistency is key in personal branding. Ensure that your message, values, and tone remain consistent across various platforms, whether it's social media, networking events, or professional engagements. Consistency builds trust and strengthens your brand identity.

4. Building Your Narrative: Craft a compelling story that reflects your journey, experiences, and aspirations. Your narrative should resonate with your audience, evoke emotions, and establish a genuine connection. Share stories that highlight your expertise and showcase your personality.

5. <u>Visual Identity:</u> While personal branding is primarily about your character and expertise, visual elements such as your appearance, online presence, and professional materials (like business cards or websites) also play a role. Ensure that these visual representations align with your brand's message.

Cultivating Your Personal Brand

1. <u>Content Creation and Sharing:</u> Share your knowledge, insights, and experiences through various mediums like blogs, videos, or podcasts. Create content that educates, inspires, or entertains your audience while showcasing your expertise.

2. <u>Networking and Relationship Building:</u> Build meaningful connections within your industry or community. Engage in networking events, conferences, and online forums to connect with like-minded individuals. Authentic relationships are invaluable in building a strong personal brand.

3. <u>Continuous Learning and Adaptability:</u> Stay updated with industry trends, sharpen your skills, and remain adaptable. Embrace continuous learning to stay relevant and showcase your growth, contributing to your personal brand's evolution.

By understanding and leveraging these key elements, you can cultivate a powerful personal brand that resonates with your audience and opens doors to numerous opportunities.

In this industry, where competition is fierce and opportunities are abundant, the key to success often lies in effective branding and the ability to stand out from the crowd. It is crucial to your success to build a compelling brand identity and strategies to differentiate yourself in the network marketing or affiliate marketing arena.

Every successful network marketer has a story that resonates with their audience. Your brand story should evoke emotions, connect with people on a personal level, and communicate your journey, struggles, and triumphs. Whether it's overcoming obstacles or achieving success, your narrative should inspire and engage others, creating a genuine connection that goes beyond mere product promotion.

Motherhood and Business - Balancing Act

In the dynamic spread of network and affiliate marketing, mothers have carved a unique path to success, balancing the demands of family life while nurturing thriving businesses. For moms juggling familial responsibilities and business aspirations, effective time management is crucial. Embrace strategies like creating schedules, setting priorities, and allocating specific time slots for both family commitments and business endeavors. Utilize tools and apps that assist in organizing tasks, enabling you to make the most of your valuable time.

As a mom engaged in network or affiliate marketing, your story is a powerful asset. Share your journey, challenges, and victories authentically. Embrace your role as a relatable figure and connect with others through your experiences. Highlight how your products or services have positively impacted your life as a mother, fostering trust and genuine connections with your audience.

In a digitally-driven era, harnessing the potential of online platforms is essential. Utilize social media, blogs, or websites to showcase your products, share valuable content, and engage with your audience. Leverage these platforms to build a community, offer support, and establish yourself as a knowledgeable resource in your niche.

Network and affiliate marketing thrives on relationships. As a mom, your nurturing instincts can be invaluable in cultivating meaningful connections. Attend networking events, engage in online forums, and participate in local community gatherings to expand your network. Building genuine relationships fosters trust and lays the foundation for long-term success.

Maintaining a balance between business endeavors and family life is fundamental for sustainable success. Practice self-care, set boundaries, and recognize the importance of downtime. A well-rested and rejuvenated mom is better equipped to handle the demands of both personal and professional spheres.

As a mom engaged in this industry, you serve as a role model not only for your children but also for aspiring entrepreneurs. Lead by example to showcase resilience, determination, and the rewards of hard work. Empower other moms by sharing your insights, providing mentorship, and creating a supportive community that fosters growth and success.

The landscape of the industry is ever-changing. Stay adaptable and open to learning. Embrace new technologies, strategies, and industry trends. Continuously seek personal and professional development opportunities to stay ahead in the game.

Moms in network and affiliate marketing possess a unique blend of nurturing skills, resilience, and determination that can pave the way for remarkable success. Through unlocking your personal brand and embracing time management, authenticity, online platforms, relationship-building, and adaptability, moms can thrive in this industry while enriching the lives of their families and communities.

JOIN THE MOVEMENT!

#MOMMAGIC

Mom Magic Movement

With The Inspired & Profitable Mompreneur

The Inspired & Profitable Mompreneur was created by Angela Bell, to serve the needs she saw and experienced as a mom; the need for time, financial freedom, and flexibility. She is the podcast host of the *Inspired & Profitable Mompreneur Podcast*, Amazon best-selling author, and motivational speaker who travels the world. Angela is the movement creator of #MomMagic, created to empower moms around the world to live their best life, and use their power to create a better world! The Inspired & Profitable Mompreneur educates, celebrates, and empowers Moms globally.

THE
INSPIRED & PROFITABLE
MOMPRENEUR
A community of Moms improving their lives, their communities and the world!

Looking to Join Us in our Next Anthology

or Publish YOUR Own?

The Inspired & Profitable Mompreneur offers full-service publishing, marketing, book tours, and campaign services. For more information, contact angela@angelabell.ca

We are always looking for women who want to share their stories and expertise and feature their businesses on our podcasts, in our books, and in our magazines.

www.ingramcontent.com/pod-product-compliance
Lightning Source LLC
Chambersburg PA
CBHW070946120626
46546CB00004B/1580